PHARMACOLOGY

HYPERTENSION

MEMORIZE DRUGS IN SECONDS...

BY FIRSTLY UNDERSTANDING HOW CONDITION PRESENTS,

HOW DRUGS WORK, MAIN SIDE-EFFECTS, CURRENT GUIDELINES, KEY POINTS AND VISUAL REVIEW MATERIAL INCLUDING IMAGES, TABLES & CONCEPT MAPS

+ COMPLEMENTARY VIDEOS ON YOUTUBE

BY J. CONSTANTINO

J. CONSTANTINO

Copyright © 2019 by J. Constantino

All rights reserved. No part of this publication may be reproduced, distributed, or transmitted in any form or by any means, including photocopying, recording, or other electronic or mechanical methods, without the prior written permission of the publisher, except in the case of brief quotations embodied in critical reviews and certain other noncommercial uses permitted by copyright law. For permission requests, write to the publisher, addressed "Attention: Permissions Coordinator," at the address below.

Flat 5 Thomas Court

65 London Road

Canterbury, Kent, UK. CT2 8JZ

Published by **Kindle direct** publishing

Ordering Information:

Title "**HYPERTENSION: EASY PEASY PHARMACOLOGY**" by **J. CONSTANTINO**

On **www.amazon.com**

THIS BOOK STRIVES TO BRING YOU A STRUCTURED LEARNING PATH ON PHARMACOLOGY BY PROVIDING YOU A **COMPLETE & SIMPLIFIED OVERVIEW ON THE PHARMACOLOGY AND PHARMACOTHERAPY** OF
HYPERTENSION

WE WILL GO THROUGH IT STEP BY STEP AND USING SIMPLE WRITING, KEY NOTES, EXPLANATIONS, DESIGNED ILLUSTRATIONS AND YET SHORT VIDEOS ON YOUTUBE

IF YOU ARE A STUDENT IT WILL HELP YOU TO ESTABLISH KEY POINTS, EXPLAIN 'WHY' AND GET A MORE VISUAL AND INTERACTIVE 'FULL PICTURE' OF THE HYPERTENSION AND ITS DRUG THERAPY.

IF YOU ARE AN HEALTH PROFESSIONAL, IT WILL REFRESH YOUR KNOWLEDGE AND UPDATE WITH THE LAST GUIDANCE OUT THERE

✓

SOME TIPS BEFORE STARTING

LEARNING IS MADE OF
COMPLEMENTARY ACTIONS AND THIS BOOK
WANTS YOU TO

NOT ONLY **READ**

BUT ALSO **WRITE**

DRAW, DESIGN

LISTEN

J. CONSTANTINO

WATCH
VISUAL LEARNING IS POWERFUL

RELAX. OUR BRAIN
NEEDS
SHORT BREAKS

REFLECT ON IT AND REVIEW..

REPEAT

REPEAT

& HAVE FUN!

J. CONSTANTINO

CLINICAL PHARMACIST

Focused on pharmacology, pharmacotherapy, clinical pharmacy, current clinical guidelines & advances in pharmacology related fields.

Currently working as a clinical pharmacist in the UK, and in parallel, I do intend to reach other health professionals and also students. For that, I dedicate some spare time writing e-books, handbooks, and producing videos for YouTube, because learning is not only reading but much more than that...

EASY PEASY PHARMACOLOGY aims at passing on information to you in an innovative, easy & appealing way, contrasting with the classic textbooks (or *bibles*) we all study or studied from.

LEARNING PATH
HYPERTENSION

STAGE BY STAGE

This book focus on hypertension (HT) - high blood pressure (BP) - and stage by stage the health condition is explained, put into tables, drawn, reviewed and further seen from different angles to complement it.

In this sense, HT should be overall better understood step by step. The learning path that I created for you is fully presented on the next page. Take a look at it, as the path will progressively be paved until you reach the end of the last stage.

I am confident HT will be a lot easier and make more sense despite of being a complex condition & the large number of different drug classes that involves.

YOUTUBE Easy Peasy Pharmacology
https://www.youtube.com/watch?v=w3i04WGddfg

HYPERTENSION

STAGE BY STAGE LEARNING PATH

STAGE 1
BP CONCEPTS AND **HYPERTENSION PATHOPHYSIOLOGY**

↓

STAGE 2
DIFFERENT CLASSES OF **ANTIHYPERTENSIVE DRUGS**

↓

STAGE 3
CLINICAL GUIDELINES ON TREATMENT LINES

↓

STAGE 4
DRUGS OF CHOICE WHEN **CONCOMITANT DISEASES**

↓

STAGE 5
DRUGS OF CHOICE FOR **SPECIAL POPULATIONS**

READY?

C'MON

LET'S GET IT STARTED.

J. CONSTANTINO

HYPERTENSION

HYPERTENSION

LEARNING PATH FOR HYPERTENSION

STAGE BY STAGE
this is the plan

BP concepts and HT **pathophysiology**

↓

Different classes of **antihypertensive drugs**

↓

Clinical guidelines on treatment lines

↓

Drugs of choice when **concomitant diseases**

↓

Drugs of choice for **special populations**

STAGE 1

J. CONSTANTINO

HYPERTENSION

STAGE BY STAGE LEARNING PATH

STAGE 1
BP CONCEPTS AND HT PATHOPHYSIOLOGY

↓

STAGE 2
DIFFERENT CLASSES OF **ANTIHYPERTENSIVE DRUGS**

↓

STAGE 3
CLINICAL GUIDELINES ON TREATMENT LINES

↓

STAGE 4
DRUGS OF CHOICE WHEN **CONCOMITANT DISEASES**

↓

STAGE 5
DRUGS OF CHOICE FOR **SPECIAL POPULATIONS**

HYPERTENSION

STAGE 1

BP CONCEPTS & HT PATHOPHISIOLOGY

- PATHOPHISIOLOGY CONCEPTS
- CARDIAC OUTPUT
- BLOOD VOLUME
- SYSTEMIC VASCULAR RESISTANCE
- HT CLASSIFICATION
- RISK FACTORS FOR BP
- DRUGS THAT MIGHT INCREASE BP
- IMPORTANT NOTES ON DIAGNOSIS
- **+ COMPLEMENTARY VIDEOS ON YOUTUBE**

J. CONSTANTINO

So, first things first!

Prior to presenting the pharmacology and pharmacotherapy in HYPERTENSION (HT) – a quick overview on pathophysiology.

There are particular **factors** - such as cardiac output, blood volume and systemic vascular resistance - **that have impact on blood pressure.** It is key to make easier the understanding of these factors since antihypertensive drugs act by modifying these factors.

The **classification of HT** is also described, where it is important to clearly understand the differences between primary HT and secondary HT.

In addition, **risk factors for HT development** are covered as well as some drugs that can increase the BP. Although this book is indeed focused on drugs that make HT to decrease, there are also drugs that can make the opposite. Sometimes a simple anti-inflammatory drug can be the cause for high blood pressure.

Finally, brief notes regarding **HT diagnosis** are also discussed at the end of this first chapter.

HYPERTENSION
PATHOPHYSIOLOGY CONCEPTS

> **YOUTUBE** Easy Peasy Pharmacology
> https://www.youtube.com/watch?v=CxbqrOT2XYM

Hypertension (HT) is a **heterogeneous disorder** where persistent arterial blood pressure (BP) is elevated.

Before going any further, it cannot be forgotten that:
BP is detrimental for perfusion of body tissues
↓
In order to feed our tissues, **relatively high amount of pressure** is needed so that **blood reaches ALL our tissues**.

> The problem or condition – hypertension –
> ONLY arises if this BP is
> HIGHER than certain values

↓
BP is mainly product of cardiac output and systemic vascular resistance, and blood volume, which will be further detailed.

- BP is then dependent on the above mentioned 3 main factors → hence anti-hypertensive drugs will act on altering them:
  ↓
  1) cardiac output
  2) blood volume
  3) systemic vascular resistance (SVR)

That being said, keep the following table in mind for factors affecting the BP, as well as the meaning of each **of them** briefly described on the next pages.

BLOOD PRESSURE DEPENDS ON		
CARDIAC OUTPUT	BLOOD VOLUME	SYSTEMIC VASCULAR RESISTANCE

This concepts are essential to understand the mechanism of action of each drug, so that this table will be found through the book to highlight by which mechanism(s) each antihypertensive drugs acts.

CARDIAC OUTPUT

The CARDIAC OUTPUT depends on HEART RATE and STROKE VOLUME.

Mathematically, this is modelled by:

CARDIAC OUTPUT = HEART RATE x STROKE VOLUME

CARDIAC OUTPUT is the amount of blood pumped by the heart through the cardiovascular system in 1 minute.

- HEART RATE is the number of heart beats per minute ***60-100 when resting

- STROKE VOLUME corresponds to the amount of blood that is pumped by the left ventricle in one contraction

Anything that makes **cardiac output decrease** also cause BP reduction as there will be ↓ **pressure on the walls**.

CURIOSITY
A normal adult has an **average CARDIAC OUTPUT of ~ 5 litres of blood per minute**.

BLOOD VOLUME

Blood volume, *i.e.* the amount of blood,
also determines the pressure on the vessels walls

↓

and therefore
blood volume influences BP

↓

in a way that:

↑ **blood volume** (e.g. due to water retention): ↑ **BP**

↓ **blood volume** (e.g. due to excessive sweating): ↓ **BP**

People who constantly eat **salty food** tend to present **water retention** due to high salt intake, having therefore their **BP increased**

↑ Na^+ in blood, ↑ H_2O in blood
↑ blood volume
↑ **BP**

SYSTEMIC VASCULAR RESISTANCE

The Systemic Vascular Resistance **(SVR)** is the last factor to highlight that also affects the BP.

It refers to the **resistance that needs to be overcome in order to push the blood through** the cardiovascular system and **keep the blood flowing.**

- The plasma and blood cells experience a certain degree of resistance when contacting with the vessel walls.

SVR depends on:
- **blood vessel diameter**
- **blood viscosity** (including amount of cholesterol)
- **total length of the vessel**

- In general, smaller vessel diameter, higher blood viscosity, and longer vessels increase SVR.

The **more resistance** is present in the blood vessels, the **more pressure** will be **needed to keep the blood flowing.** = higher BP.

We have just learnt the 3 main factors that determine the BP, which are: CARDIAC OUTPUT, BLOOD VOLUME, SYSTEMIC VASCULAR RESISTANCE

(...) Now, we can move forward onto the rest of stage 1 section which includes:

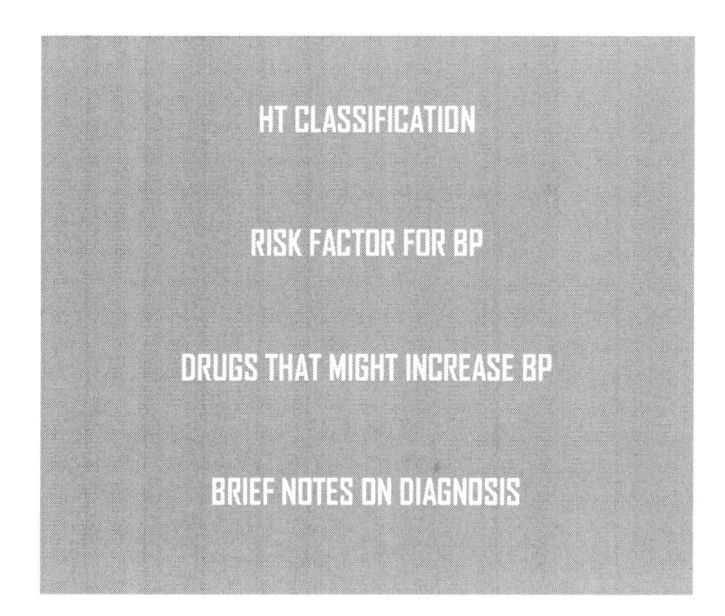

HT CLASSIFICATION

RISK FACTOR FOR BP

DRUGS THAT MIGHT INCREASE BP

BRIEF NOTES ON DIAGNOSIS

LET'S GET IT STARTED!

HT can be classified as PRIMARY or SECONDARY

WHAT ARE THE DIFFERENCES?

≠

PRIMARY	SECONDARY
• **> 90 %** of cases (MOST CASES)	• **< 10%** of cases
CAUSE: Unknown ↓ Results from an underlying pathophysiologic mechanism of unknown cause.	CAUSE: Underlying known condition(s) are present increasing the blood pressure ↓ **Chronic kidney disease** or **renovascular disease** are the most common Other possible ones are Cushing's syndrome, Pheochromocytoma Obstructive sleep apnea Primary hyperaldosteronism & Hyperthyroidism)

Blood pressure problems can lead ultimately to death. BP is indeed one of the easiest risk factors to modify in order to **prevent strokes, cardiovascular events** or **renal failure** that could end up in **death.**

> The higher the BP is the more likely premature death becomes.
>
> Main causes of death for HT patients:
>
> Strokes
>
> Cardiovascular (CV) events
>
> Renal failure

So, in other words, hypertension does not kill directly but it can lead to death as hypertension can contribute to strokes, CV events and renal failure.

RISK FACTORS FOR DEVELOPING HT

There are several risk factors for developing HT:

RISK FACTORS

- Age
- Ethnicity (more common in patients of black African/Caribbean descent)
- Obesity
- Lack of exercise
- Excess salt intake
- Stress
- Diabetes Mellitus
- Chronic Kidney Disease
- Sleep apnea
- Intake of alcohol

Not only these risk factors can increase BP but ALSO SOME DRUGS!

Let's repeat it to stress this notion - there are indeed **ALSO drugs** that can make BP to increase, meaning that when talking to a patient it is crucial to have the **full picture including their medication history**!

DRUGS that may cause increased BP

- Corticosteroids
- Nonsteriodal anti-inflammatory drugs **(NSAIDs)***
- Oral contraceptives containing estrogens
- Decongestants
- 5-HT1 receptor agonists (e.g. sumatriptan, rizatriptan)
- Ciclosporine
- Recreational drugs (e.g. cocaine, amphetamines, ecstasy)
- Venlafaxine
- Tacrolimus

* How NSAIDs can cause high BP?

As an example, a simple NSAID used chronically for any musculoskeletal condition may be the origin of **persistent high BP**.

↓

> **WHY?**
>
> NSAIDs significantly decrease production of prostaglandins, & the prostaglandins lead to vasodilation.
>
> So,
>
> when prostaglandins are decreased by NSAIDs, the results are:
>
> ↓ **Vasodilation,** ↑ **Vasoconstriction**
>
> ↑ **Systemic Vascular Resistance**
>
> And ultimately
>
> ↑ **BP**

Many patients are not aware of the impact of NSAIDs in their BP. On many occasions, replacing NSAIDs for paracetamol can resolve a high blood pressure issue, because NSAIDs were causing increased BP in the first place.

DIAGNOSIS OF HYPERTENSION

Main sign of primary HT is **elevated BP** in physical examination of BP, as patients are usually asymptomatic initially.

CLASSIFICATION OF BP ACCORDING TO SYSTOLIC AND DIASTOLIC VALUES		
TYPE	**SYSTOLIC mmHg**	**DIASTOLIC mmHg**
Normal	<120	<80
Pre-HT	120-139	80-89
Stage 1	140-159	90-99
Stage 2	≥160	≥100
Severe HT	≥180	≥110

- ✓ If HT is not diagnosed for patients with values of BP close to 140/90 mmHg (especially for patients with factor risks), **clinic BP should be monitored** regularly - at least **annually**.

✓ **Pathologic changes** related to **heart, kidneys, peripheral blood vessels, eyes,** and **brain** may begin to be apparent – signs of modification in these organs should be prudently considered, & signs of target organ damage should be investigated for **cardiovascular risk**.

DO NOT FORGET SECONDARY HT!

Secondary HT shall ALSO be considered **where an underlying** conditions **can be present**, despite of being the case for less than 10 per cent of the cases:

↓

PRIMARY	SECONDARY
> 90 % of cases	< 10% of cases
CAUSE: Unknown Results from an underlying pathophysiologic mechanism of unknown cause.	**CAUSE: Underlying known condition(s)** are present increasing the blood pressure: **Chronic kidney disease** or **renovascular disease** are the most common. Other possible ones are Cushing's syndrome, pheochromocytoma, obstructive sleep apnea, primary hyperaldosteronism & hyperthyroidism.

For secondary HT assessment and diagnostic: **laboratory tests** should be performed.

Briefly, these laboratory tests are **listed below**

PHEOCHROMOCYTOMA INVESTIGATION
Norepinephrine (plasma)
Metanephrine (urinary)

PRIMARY ALDOSTERONISM
Aldosterone (plasma & urinary)

RENOVASCULAR DISEASE
Renin activity (plasma)
Captopril stimulation test
Renin (renal vein)
Renal artery angiography.

STAGE 2

HYPERTENSION

STAGE BY STAGE LEARNING PATH

STAGE 1
BP CONCEPTS AND **HT PATHOPHYSIOLOGY**

↓

STAGE 2
DIFFERENT CLASSES OF **ANTIHYPERTENSIVE DRUGS**

↓

STAGE 3
CLINICAL GUIDELINES ON TREATMENT LINES

↓

STAGE 4
DRUGS OF CHOICE WHEN **CONCOMITANT DISEASES**

↓

STAGE 5
DRUGS OF CHOICE FOR **SPECIAL POPULATIONS**

HYPERTENSION

STAGE 2

DIFFERENT CLASSES OF ANTIHYPERTENSIVE DRUGS

ANGIOTENSIN-CONVERTING ENZYME (ACE) INHIBITORS

ANGIOTENSIN II RECEPTOR BLOCKERS (ARBs)

CALCIUM CHANNEL BLOCKERS (CCBs)

2 TYPES: DIHYDROPYRIDINES | NON-DIHYDROPYRIDINES

DIURETICS

4 TYPES: THIAZIDES | LOOP | POTASSIUM SPARING | ALDOSTERONE ANTAGONISTS

BETA-BLOCKERS

α1- RECEPTOR BLOCKERS

+ COMPLEMENTARY VIDEOS ON YOUTUBE

Let's talk about drugs.

After learning about the main BP concepts and HT pathophysiology, the antihypertensive drugs are presented one by one.

Firstly the **mechanism of action** of each drug is introduced. Then we will look into a bit further detail into each class, regarding **key points** to keep in mind, **side effects** and **cautions** to have.

And because reviewing is key for learning, the main points are reviewed at the end of this chapter.

> **YOUTUBE** Easy Peasy Pharmacology
>
> https://www.youtube.com/watch?v=Ebe_8l7Gpk4&t=13s
>
> https://www.youtube.com/watch?v=Wam8iWvp74E

ANTIHYPERTENSIVE DRUGS

These are the different classes of antihypertensive drugs:

ANGIOTENSIN-CONVERTING ENZYME (ACE) INHIBITORS

ANGIOTENSIN II RECEPTOR BLOCKERS (ARBs)

CALCIUM CHANNEL BLOCKERS (CCBs)

DIURETICS

BETA-BLOCKERS

α1- RECEPTOR BLOCKERS

ANTIHYPERTENSIVE DRUGS

Please note there are even more classes of drugs that can have antihypertensive effect, but they are hardly prescribed for hypertension conditions.

To start with, I suggest to look into the **mechanism of action** of each drug:

ANGIOTENSIN-CONVERTING ENZYME (ACE) INHIBITORS

ANGIOTENSIN II RECEPTOR BLOCKERS (ARBs)

CALCIUM CHANNEL BLOCKERS (CCBs)

DIURETICS

BETA-BLOCKERS

α1- RECEPTOR BLOCKERS

ANTIHYPERTENSIVE DRUGS

ANGIOTENSIN-CONVERTING ENZYME (ACE) INHIBITORS

ACE inhibitors act by blocking the conversion of angiotensin I to angiotensin II (a potent vasoconstrictor and stimulator of aldosterone production).
As a result, ACE inhibitors act by mainly:
- ↓ **vasoconstriction**
- ↓ **aldosterone release**
- ↓ **BP**

ANGIOTENSIN II RECEPTOR BLOCKERS (ARBs)

ARBs act by direct blockage of angiotensin receptors where angiotensin II binds, thus ↓ angiotensin II main effects:
- ↓ **vasoconstriction**
- ↓ **aldosterone release**
- ↓ **BP**

CALCIUM CHANNEL BLOCKERS (CCBs) 2 TYPES:
DIHYDROPYRIDINES & NON-DIHYDROPYRIDINES

Extracellular calcium (Ca^{2+}) is essential to enter inside the muscle cells and make them to contract. CCBs act by inhibiting calcium channels and thereby reducing the amount of Ca^{2+} to enter into the muscle cells.

Depending on its specificity, CCBs act on ≠ tissues and lead to ≠ outcomes:

1) vascular smooth muscle: **vasodilation**

2) myocardium: ↓ **in contractility**, ↓ **in heart rate**

3) cardiac conduction tissues: ↓ **in contractility**, ↓ **in heart rate**

DIURETICS

4 TYPES: THIAZIDES | LOOP | POTASSIUM SPARING | ALDOSTERONE ANTAGONISTS

Diuretics act by ↑ diuresis

↓ **salt and water retention in the kidney**

Basically, as a result:

↓ **circulating blood volume**

↓ **cardiac output**

Then: ↓ **BP**

BETA-BLOCKERS

β-blockers act by blocking β-receptors.
By blocking the **β1** receptors on the heart, the results are:
- ↓ **heart rate**
- ↓ **contractility**
- ↓ **cardiac output**
- ↓ **BP**

α1- RECEPTOR BLOCKERS

α1-receptor blockers act by inhibiting catecholamine uptake by α1 receptors in the smooth muscle of peripheral vasculature, leading to its relaxation and vasodilation:
- ↓ **systemic vascular resistance (SVR)**
- ↓ **BP**

ANTIHYPERTENSIVE DRUGS

There are different mechanism of action that can result in blood pressure reduction.

1 ACE INHIBITORS

ACE inhibitors act by blocking the conversion of angiotensin I to angiotensin II - a potent vasoconstrictor and stimulator of aldosterone production.
As a result, ACE inhibitors act by mainly:
- ↓ vasoconstriction
- ↓ aldosterone release
- ↓ BP

2 ARB

ARBs act by direct blockage of angiotensin receptors where angiotensin II binds.
Similarly to ACE inhibitors, ARBs ↓ angiotensin II main effects:
- ↓ vasoconstriction
- ↓ aldosterone release
- ↓ BP

3 CCB

CCBs act on ≠ tissues and then lead to ≠ outcomes accordingly:
1) if acting on vascular smooth muscle: vasodilation
2) if acting on myocardium: ↓ in contractility, ↓ in heart rate
3) if acting on cardiac conduction tissues: ↓ in contractility, ↓ in heart rate

4. DIURETICS

**4 DIFFERENT TYPES:
THIAZIDES | LOOP |
POTASSIUM SPARING |
ALDOSTERONE ANTAGONISTS**

Diuretics act by
↑ diuresis
↓ salt and water retention in the kidney

Basically, as a result:

↓ circulating blood volume
↓ cardiac output
Then: ↓ BP

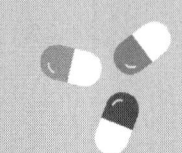

5. BETA-BLOCKERS

β-blockers act by blocking β-receptors

By blocking the β1 receptors on the heart, the results are:

↓ heart rate
↓ contractility
↓ cardiac output
↓ BP

6. ALFA-1 RECEPTOR BLOCKERS

α1 receptor blockers act by inhibiting catecholamine uptake by α1 receptors in the smooth muscle of peripheral vasculature, leading to its relaxation and vasodilation:

↓ systemic vascular resistance (SVR)

ANTIHYPERTENSIVE DRUGS

Now let's look into more detail at each class of these drugs, one by one.

ANGIOTENSIN-CONVERTING ENZYME (ACE) INHIBITORS

Ramipril, lisinopril, captopril, enalapril, lisinopril, perindopril, trandolapril, quinapril (...)

ACE inhibitors act by blocking the conversion of angiotensin I to angiotensin II (a potent vasoconstrictor and stimulator of aldosterone production).

As a result, ACE inhibitors lower BP by mainly
- ↓ vasoconstriction
- ↓ aldosterone release

Basically, taking into account the table:

BLOOD PRESSURE ↓		
↓ CARDIAC OUTPUT	↓ BLOOD VOLUME	↓↓ SYSTEMIC VASCULAR RESISTANCE

- **ACE inhibitors** are a **first-line drug** used in patients **under 55 years of age**.

- Can increase potassium levels: ↑ K⁺ called hyperkalemia. Hyperkalemia is more likely in patients with chronic kidney disease or those on potassium-sparing diuretics, potassium supplements, ARBs or direct renin inhibitors.

- Persistent dry, irritant cough may occur in up to 20% of patients and it happens due to inhibition of bradykinin* degradation.

What is *bradykinin?

*bradykinin is a bronchoconstrictor substance. Normally the enzyme ACE is responsible for its degradation. Thus bradykinin can get accumulated in airways in patients taking ACE inhibitors, causing dry persistent cough.

↓

As an alternative, to the patient who suffer from the dry cough side effect, ARBs are normally prescribed.

So it is essential to keep in mind that ARBs are the alternative for those who present **dry cough** associated with ACE inhibitors.

- Acute hypotension can occur at onset of ACE inhibitors therapy → so **low dose with slow dose titration** should be performed, especially in elderly, patients on other antihypertensive drugs, or those with heart failure (HF) exacerbation.

- **Acute renal failure** is a serious possible side effect - although it is rare, patients with pre-existing kidney diseases are considered at higher risk.

- ACE inhibitors are completely contraindicated (CI) in **pregnancy** as they can lead to major congenital malformations in fetus, renal failure and death in infants.

- Due to **inhibition of vasoconstriction on efferent arterioles**, glomerular filtration rate (GFR) often decreases. Creatinine levels tend to be slightly higher but normally no more than 1mg/dL – if larger increases than that, therapy should be reviewed (stopped/reduced)

- **Angioedema** (lip and tongue swelling and possible breathing difficulties) is a very serious complication that occurs in less than 1% of patients - those of black African and Caribbean origin are at higher risk of angioedema complications.

ANGIOTENSIN II RECEPTOR BLOCKERS (ARBs)

Candesartan, irbesartan, losartan, olmesartan, telmisartan, valsartan (...)

ARBs act by direct blockage of angiotensin receptors where angiotensin II binds, thus ↓ **angiotensin II effects**.

Therefore ARBs cause:
- ↓ **vasoconstriction**
- ↓ **aldosterone release**
- ↓ **sympathetic activation**
- ↓ **antidiuretic hormone release**
- ↓ **constriction of efferent arterioles of the glomerulus**

BLOOD PRESSURE ↓		
↓ CARDIAC OUTPUT	↓ BLOOD VOLUME	↓↓ SYSTEMIC VASCULAR RESISTANCE

- Unlike ACE inhibitors, ARBs do not block bradykinin degradation, so dry cough is not possible side effect which is an advantage of ARBs. Many patients are changed to ARBs as alternative to ACE inhibitors when presenting dry persistent cough.

- However there is also a disadvantage of ARBs over ACE inhibitors. Some studies suggest that ARBs may not be as good at lowering the BP since bradykinin may be important for antihypertensive effects of ACE inhibitors, and also important to reduce myocyte hypertrophy and fibrosis.

- ARBs have positively the lowest incidence of side effects when compared with the other antihypertensive drugs - they do not cause dry cough associated with ACE inhibitors as mentioned above, but like ACE inhibitors they can also cause ↑ **K⁺ (hyperkalemia), acute hypotension** and **renal insufficiency**

- ARBs should not be used in pregnancy like ACE inhibitors x **CI in pregnancy**

CALCIUM CHANNEL BLOCKERS (CCBs)

2 TYPES
DIHYDROPYRIDINES & NON-DIHYDROPYRIDINES

Extracellular calcium (Ca^{2+}) is essential to enter inside the muscle cells and make them to contract.

CCBs act by inhibiting calcium channels and thereby reducing the amount of Ca^{2+} to enter into the muscle cells.

There are ≠ types of CCBs with ≠ specificity, meaning that different CCBs are specific for ≠ tissues: 1) vascular smooth muscle 2) myocardium 3) cardiac conduction tissues

↓

Leading to ≠ outcomes depending on their greater specificity.

If they act on:

1) **vascular smooth tissue**: then, there is vasodilation
2) **myocardium**: ↓ contractility, ↓ heart rate
3) **cardiac conduction tissues**: ↓ contractility, ↓ heart rate

> **KEY POINT**
> Keep in mind that CCBs are 1st line antihypertensive agents in patients aged 55yrs or over.

There are **2 types of CCBs**, as mentioned before:

1) DIHYDROPYRIDINES

   Amlodipine, nifedipine, felodipine, nicardipine

2) NON-DIHYDROPYRIDINES

   Diltiazem, Verapamil

Let's see what the differences are between them...

1) DIHYDROPYRIDINES CCBs

Amlodipine, nifedipine, felodipine, nicardipine

- Dihydropyridine CCBs have greater selectivity for 1) **vascular smooth muscle.**

↓

HOW DOES IT WORK?

By blocking Ca^{2+} to enter this smooth muscle cells, there is muscle relaxation

that leads consequently to:

Vasodilation

↓ **systemic vascular resistance (SVR)**

↓ **BP**

- This first type of CCBs (**dihydropyridines**) are **preferred for treatment of hypertension.**

- **Postural hypotension** can happen as side effect - it is the most dangerous especially for elderly people.

That being said, their main side effect relates to possible **REFLEX SYMPATHETIC ACTIVATION**.

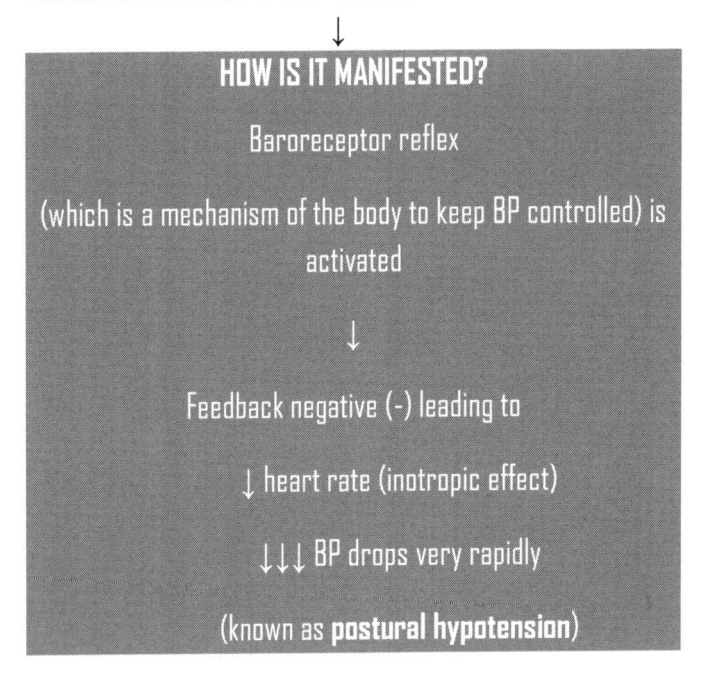

↓

HOW IS IT MANIFESTED?

Baroreceptor reflex

(which is a mechanism of the body to keep BP controlled) is activated

↓

Feedback negative (-) leading to

↓ heart rate (inotropic effect)

↓↓↓ BP drops very rapidly

(known as **postural hypotension**)

↓

Important note: This side effect is more common with nifedipine use. So **nifedipine is less preferred than amlodipine or felodipine to treat HT.** There is lower risk of reflex sympathetic activation and sudden postural hypotension with amlodipine or felodipine.

- Other possible side effects of dihydropyridines CCBs are: **flushing, headache, peripheral oedema, dizziness,** and **gingival hyperplasia** (manifested by swollen gums)

2) NON-DIHYDROPYRIDINES CCBs

Diltiazem, Verapamil

Verapamil:
Slows **nodal conduction**, leading to

↓ heart rate (negative inotropic effect)

↓ BP

$$\neq$$
Whereas,

Diltiazem:
Acts mainly on **coronary vasculature**
Therefore diltiazem still decreases nodal conduction and heart rate but to a lower extension than verapamil.

- These non-dihydropyridine CCBs (diltiazem and verapamil) can cause cardiac conduction abnormalities (e.g. bradycardia and heart failure (HF).

- Verapamil (least selective CCB) can block the Ca^{2+} channels on smooth muscle present in the gastro-intestinal (GI) system so it can lead to constipation (around 7% of patient).

- They may be used in patients with hypertension and concurrent arrhythmias (e.g. AF) or angina, due to their additional effects on the myocardium and HR.

DIURETICS

Diuretics act by ↓ **salt and water retention** in the kidney, ↑ **diuresis.** Basically, as a result:

↓ circulating blood volume

↓ cardiac output

Then: ↓ **BP**

THERE ARE 4 ≠ CLASSES OF DIURETICS

1. THIAZIDES

Hydrochlorothiazide, bendroflumethiazide, indapamide, chortalidone

- Thiazides reduce the reabsorption of Na^+ and H_2O at the distal convoluted tubule in kidneys, so more Na^+ and Cl^- are expelled out and H_2O follows it.
  ↓H_2O ↓Blood volume (↓cardiac output): ↓BP

- Thiazides can cause
- hypokalaemia ↓K^+
- hyponatraemia ↓Na^+ (rarely)

- dehydration $\downarrow H_2O$

    So serum electrolytes and renal function should be monitored regularly during treatment.

- $\downarrow K^+$, $\downarrow Mg^{2+}$ may cause muscle fatigue and cramps

- Thiazides and thiazide-like diuretics are also vasodilators.

- Thiazides (especially hydrochlorothiazide and bendroflumethiazide) can also cause:
- Hyperglycemia ($\uparrow$serum glucose)
- Hyperuricemia ($\uparrow$uric acid in blood)
- Dyslipidemia ($\uparrow$serum lipids)

    So should be avoided in patients with diabetes, gout and dyslipidemia.

- Low-dose thiazide-like diuretics (e.g. indapamide and chlortalidone) should be used in preference to the first thiazide diuretics (bendroflumethiazide and hydrochlorothiazide).

2. LOOP DIURETICS

Furosemide, bumetanide

- Loop diuretics are the most potent diuretics, inhibiting the reabsorption of Na^+, Cl^- and H_2O in the kidneys
  ↑↑diuresis
  ↓↓H_2O in body ↓Blood volume
  (↓cardiac output): ↓BP

- Loop diuretics have less effect on serum lipids and glucose, BUT hypokalaemia ↓↓ K^+ is more pronounced.

- For this reason, they are not ideal for HT treatment unless relief of oedema is required

- ↓K^+, ↓Mg^{2+} may cause muscle fatigue and cramps

3. POTASSIUM SPARING

Amiloride, triamterene

- Potassium sparing diuretics are weak antihypertensive drugs. But they have an additive effect in lowering the BP and may be useful to counteract the loss of K^+, and even Mg^{2+} promoted by thiazide or loop diuretics.

- ↑K^+: May cause hyperkalaemia, should be used with caution if patient is taking ACE inhibitors, ARB, direct renin inhibitor or K^+ supplements. Also caution in patients with kidney conditions or diabetes

4. ALDOSTERONE ANTAGONISTS

Spironolactone, Eplerenone

- By resembling the aldosterone hormone, they act as competitive inhibitors, preventing the aldosterone binding on the distal portion of the renal tubule.

- As a result, there is increased Na^+ and H_2O excretion, and reduced K^+ excretion (also classified as potassium sparing diuretic like amiloride and triamterene).

- Spironolactone may cause gynecomastia in up to 10% of patients
- Eplerenone has an increased risk of ↑K^+ hyperkalaemia so it is contraindicated in patients with renal problems or type 2 diabetes with proteinuria.

BETA-BLOCKERS

- β-blockers act by blocking β-receptors. By blocking the β1 receptors on the heart, the results are:

  ↓ **heart rate**

  ↓ **contractility**

  ↓ **cardiac output:** ↓BP

  Depending on their selectivity some β-blockers may block other receptors besides β1 as detailed below.

1) SELECTIVE BETA-BLOCKERS

Atenolol, bisoprolol, metoprolol

- Selective β-blockers are then cardioselective, which means they bind to β1 receptors more strongly than to β2 or β3 receptors. β1 receptors are present mainly on the heart tissues (and also kidneys), so the main effects are:

  ↓ heart rate

  ↓ contractility

  ↓ cardiac output: ↓BP

- Note that:
- β2 receptors are present mainly on 1) vascular smooth muscle, 2) skeletal muscle and 3) lungs
- β3 receptors are present on fat cells.

- Also note that cardioselectivity is only present at low doses, and these effects are lost at higher doses.
- Low doses of selective β-blockers have lower effect on β2 or β3 receptors, so they are LESS LIKELY to cause:
- Bronchoconstriction (when β2 are blocked on lungs)
- Vasoconstriction (when β2 are blocked on vascular smooth muscle)

As a result, they are safer for patients with asthma, chronic obstructive pulmonary disease (COPD), diabetes or peripheral artery disease (PAD).

2) NON-SELECTIVE BETA-BLOCKERS

Propranolol, pindolol, acebutolol

- Non-Selective β-blockers can bind to β1, β2, and β3 receptors.
- **Non-selective β-blockers** are not recommended for patients with **asthma, chronic obstructive pulmonary disease (COPD), diabetes or peripheral artery disease (PAD).**
  ↓
  WHY? By blocking β2 receptors on lungs and muscle tissues can result in:
- Bronchoconstriction
- Vasoconstriction
- Cold extremities (resultant from β2 blockage in arteriolar smooth muscle)

PHARMACOKINETIC DIFFERENCES

- ≠ β-blockers present major differences that may impact on choice of the appropriate β-blockers taking into account the patient pharmacokinetic differences in terms of:

- **Firt-pass metabolism and half-lives**: Propranolol and metoprolol suffer metabolised extensively; whilst atenolol and nadolol have long half-lives (however once-daily administration is still effective in some of those with shorter half-lives)

- **Lipophility**: atenolol, nadolol and sotalol are water soluble; but other β-blockers are more lipophilic so they have higher CNS penetration, and therefore they can more likely cause vivid dreams/nightmares. Therefore if a patient on β-blockers has started experiencing vivid dreams/nightmares, it may likely be related to the medication and changes to atenolol, nadolol or sotalol can be considered.

- **Elimination route:** Atenolol and nadolol are excreted renally so patient with renal insufficiency should have lower dosages.

- In general, β-blockers can cause bradycardia, conduction abnormalities, acute heart failure (HF).

> **!**
>
> **Abrupt discontinuation of β-blockers** can produce myocardial infarction, unstable angina, or even death especially in patients with coronary disease. Hence, slow reductions are advised over a period of at least 1 or 2 weeks.

α1- RECEPTOR BLOCKERS

Doxazosin, prazosin

- α1-receptor blockers act by inhibiting catecholamine uptake by α1 receptors in the smooth muscle of peripheral vasculature, leading to its relaxation and vasodilation:
  ↓ systemic vascular resistance (SVR)
  ↓ BP

- Orthostatic hypotension may occur potentially due to sudden BP drop – accompanying signs can be present such as dizziness or fainting, palpitations and even syncope

- Na^+ and H_2O retention can also appear so α1-receptor blockers used chronically should be given together with diuretics to minimize risk of edema

- For HT, α1-receptor blockers should only be given with first-line antihypertensives

Men with benign prostatic hyperplasia is a particular situation for which α1-receptor blockers can be reserved.

REVIEW OF ANTIHYPERTENSIVE DRUGS

It's time to review and summarise the classes of HT drugs discussed previously...

ANGIOTENSIN-CONVERTING ENZYME (ACE) INHIBITORS

ANGIOTENSIN II RECEPTOR BLOCKERS (ARBs)

CALCIUM CHANNEL BLOCKERS (CCBs)

DIHYDROPYRIDINES | NON-DIHYDROPYRIDINES

DIURETICS

THIAZIDES | LOOP | POTASSIUM SPARING | ALDOSTERONE ANTAGONISTS

BETA-BLOCKERS

α1- RECEPTOR BLOCKERS

ANGIOTENSIN-CONVERTING ENZYME (ACE) INHIBITORS

Ramipril, lisinopril, captopril, enalapril, lisinopril, perindopril, trandolapril, quinapril

- ACE inhibitors act by **blocking** the conversion of angiotensin I to **angiotensin II**
  OUTCOME:
- ↓ vasoconstriction (angiotensin is a potent vasoconstrictor)
- ↓ aldosterone release (angiotensin II stimulates aldosterone production)

- ACE inhibitors are a first-line drug used in patients under 55 years of age

- Can increase potassium levels (hyperkalemia). Hyperkalemia is more likely in patients with chronic kidney disease or those on potassium-sparing diuretics, potassium supplements, ARBs or direct renin inhibitors.

- Acute hypotension can occur at onset → so low dose with slow dose titration should be performed, especially in elderly, patients on other antihypertensive drugs, or those with heart failure (HF) exacerbation.

- Persistent dry, irritant cough may occur in up to 20% of patients
  (**WHY?** due to inhibition of bradykinin degradation)

- As an alternative, ARBs are normally prescribed for those who present dry cough associated with ACE inhibitors.

- Acute renal failure is a serious possible side effect - although it is rare, patients with pre-existing kidney diseases are considered at higher risk.

- ACE inhibitors are completely CI in pregnancy (**WHY?** they can lead to major congenital malformations in fetus, renal failure and death in infants)

- Due to inhibition of vasoconstriction on efferent arterioles, glomerular filtration rate (GFR) often decreases.
  Creatinine levels tend to be slightly higher but normally no more than 1mg/dL - if larger increases than that, therapy should be reviewed (stopped/reduced)

- Angioedema (lip and tongue swelling and possible breathing difficulties) is a very serious complication that occurs in less than 1% of patients
  Those of black African and Caribbean origin are at higher risk of angioedema complications

ANGIOTENSIN II RECEPTOR BLOCKERS (ARBs)

Candesartan, irbesartan, losartan, olmesartan, telmisartan, valsartan

- ARBs act by direct blockage of angiotensin receptors where angiotensin II binds, thus ↓ angiotensin II effects:
- ↓ vasoconstriction
- ↓ aldosterone release
- ↓ sympathetic activation
- ↓ antidiuretic hormone release
- ↓ constriction of efferent arterioles of the glomerulus

- Unlike ACE inhibitors, ARBs **do not block bradykinin** degradation – so there is no dry cough as possible side effect which is an advantage.

- BUT! There is also a disadvantage - ARBs may not be as good at lowering the BP
  (**WHY?** some studies suggest that bradykinin may be important for antihypertensive effects of ACE inhibitors, and also important to reduce myocyte hypertrophy and fibrosis)

- ARBs have positively the **lowest incidence of side effects** when compared with the other antihypertensive drugs

- BUT! Like ACE inhibitors they can also cause **hyperkalemia, acute hypotension & renal insufficiency**

- ARBs are **CI in pregnancy** like ACE inhibitors.

CALCIUM CHANNEL BLOCKERS (CCBs)

(2 TYPES | DIHYDROPYRIDINES & NON-DIHYDROPYRIDINES)

Extracellular calcium (Ca^{2+}) is essential to enter inside the muscle cells and make them to contract → CCBs act by inhibiting Ca^{2+} channels → ↓ the amount of Ca^{2+} to enter into the muscle cells → ↓ contraction

There are ≠ types of CCBs with ≠ specificity.
Different CCBs are specific for ≠ tissues:
1) vascular smooth muscle
2) myocardium
3) cardiac conduction tissues

leading to outcomes depending on their greater specificity:
- Vasodilation (when act on vascular smooth tissue)
- ↓ in contractility, ↓ in heart rate (when act on cardiac conduction tissues/myocardium)

CCBs are 1st line antihypertensive agents in patients aged 55yrs or over (as per NICE guidelines)

DIHYDROPYRIDINES CCBs
Amlodipine, nifedipine, felodipine, nicardipine

- Dihydropyridine CCBs have greater selectivity for vascular smooth muscle. By blocking Ca^{2+} to enter this smooth muscle cells, there is muscle relaxation that leads to vasodilation: ↓ systemic vascular resistance (SVR): ↓ BP

- This type of CCBs are **preferred for treatment of HT** than non-dihydropyridines.

- **Main side effect** relates to possible reflex sympathetic activation leading to ↓ heart rate (inotropic effect) and causes **postural hypotension** ↓↓↓BP drops rapidly (This is more common when using nifedipine and less common with amlodipine and felodipine).

- Other side effects: dizziness, headache, flushing, peripheral oedema and gingival hyperplasia (manifested by swollen gums)

NON-DIHYDROPYRIDINES CCBs
Diltiazem, Verapamil

- Verapamil slows nodal condution, leading to ↓ heart rate (negative inotropic effect): ↓ BP

- Diltiazem acts mainly on coronary vasculature and decreases nodal conduction and heart rate to a lower extension than verapamil.

- Both diltiazem and verapamil can cause cardiac conduction abnormalities (e.g. bradycardia and HF).

- Verapamil (least selective CCB) can block the Ca^{2+} channels on smooth muscle present in the GI system so it can lead to constipation (around 7% of patient).

- They may be used in patients with HT and concurrent arrhythmias (e.g. AF) or angina, due to their additional effects on the myocardium and HR.

DIURETICS

Diuretics act by ↓ salt and water retention in the kidney, ↑ diuresis.
Basically, as a result:
↓ circulating blood volume ↓ cardiac output ↓ BP

4 ≠ **CLASSES** OF DIURETICS:

**THIAZIDES
LOOP
K⁺ SPARING
ALDOSTERONE ANTAGONISTS**

THIAZIDES (DIURETICS)
Hydrochlorothiazide, bendroflumethiazide, indapamide, chortalidone

- Thiazides reduce the reabsorption of Na^+ and H_2O at the distal convoluted tubule in kidneys, so more Na^+ and Cl^- are expelled out and H_2O follows it.
  ↓H_2O ↓Blood volume (↓cardiac output): ↓BP

- Thiazides can cause

- hypokalaemia ↓K⁺
- hyponatraemia ↓Na⁺ (rarely)
- dehydration ↓H$_2$O
So serum electrolytes and renal function should be monitored regularly during treatment.

- ↓K⁺, ↓Mg^{2+} may cause muscle fatigue and cramps

- Thiazides and thiazide-like diuretics are also vasodilators.

- Thiazides (especially hydrochlorothiazide and bendroflumethiazide) can also cause:
- Hyperglycemia (↑serum glucose)
- Hyperuricemia (↑uric acid in blood)
- Dyslipidemia (↑serum lipids)

    So should be avoided in patients with diabetes, gout and dyslipidemia.

- Low-dose thiazide-like diuretics (e.g. indapamide and chlortalidone) should be used in preference to the first thiazide diuretics (bendroflumethiazide and hydrochlorothiazide).

LOOP DIURETICS
Furosemide, bumetanide

- Loop diuretics are the most potent diuretics, inhibiting the reabsorption of Na⁺, Cl⁻ and H$_2$O in the kidneys

↑↑diuresis

↓↓H_2O in body ↓Blood volume

(↓cardiac output): ↓BP

- Loop diuretics have less effect on serum lipids and glucose, BUT hypokalaemia ↓↓K^+ is more pronounced.

- For this reason, they are not ideal for HT treatment unless relief of oedema is required

- ↓K^+, ↓Mg^{2+} may cause muscle fatigue and cramps.

POTASSIUM SPARING (DIURETICS)
Amiloride, triamterene

- Potassium sparing diuretics are weak antihypertensive drugs. But they have an additive effect in lowering the BP and may be useful to counteract the loss of K^+, and even Mg^{2+} promoted by thiazide or loop diuretics.

- ↑ K^+
May cause hyperkalaemia, should be used with caution if patient is taking ACE inhibitors, ARB, direct renin inhibitor or K^+ supplements. Also caution in patients with kidney conditions or diabetes

ALDOSTERONE ANTAGONISTS
Spironolactone, Eplerenone

- By resembling the aldosterone hormone, they act as competitive inhibitors, preventing the aldosterone binding on the distal portion of the renal tubule.

- As a result, there is increased Na^+ and H_2O excretion, and reduced K^+ excretion (also classified as potassium sparing diuretic like amiloride and triamterene).

- Spironolactone may cause gynecomastia (in up to 10% of patients).

- Eplerenone has an increased risk of ↑K^+ hyperkalaemia so it is contraindicated in patients with renal problems

BETA-BLOCKERS

- Beta-blockers act by blocking β receptors. When blocking beta-1 receptors (the ones present on the heart), the results are:
  - ↓ **heart rate**
  - ↓ **contractility**
  - ↓ **cardiac output:** ↓BP

Depending on their selectivity some β-blockers may block other receptors besides β1 as detailed below

---

SELECTIVE
Atenolol, bisoprolol, metoprolol

- Selective β-blockers are then cardioselective, which means they bind to β1 receptors more strongly than to β2 or β3 receptors. β1 receptors are present mainly on the heart tissues (and also kidneys), so the main

effects are:
↓ heart rate
↓ contractility
↓ cardiac output: ↓ BP

- Note:
- β2 receptors are present mainly on 1) vascular smooth muscle, 2) skeletal muscle and 3) lungs
- β3 receptors are present on fat cells.

It should be noted that cardioselectivity is only present at low doses, and these effects are lost at higher doses. Low doses of selective β-blockers have lower effect on β2 or β3 receptors, so they are LESS LIKELY to cause:
- Bronchoconstriction (when β2 are blocked on lungs)
- Vasoconstriction (when β2 are blocked on vascular smooth muscle)
  Safer for patients with **asthma, COPD, diabetes** or **PAD.**

NON-SELECTIVE
Propranolol, pindolol, acebutolol

- Non-Selective β-blockers can bind to β1, β2, and β3 receptors.

- Non-selective β-blockers are not recommended for patients with asthma, chronic obstructive pulmonary disease (COPD), diabetes or peripheral artery disease (PAD)

As their effect by blocking β2 receptors on lungs and muscle tissues can result in:

- Bronchoconstriction
- Vasoconstriction
- Cold extremities (resultant from β2 blockage in arteriolar smooth muscle)

PHARMACOKINETIC DIFFERENCES BETWEEN β-blockers

- Firt-pass metabolism and half-lives: Propranolol and metoprolol suffer metabolised extensively
Atenolol and nadolol have long half-lives (however once-daily administration is still effective in some of those with shorter half-lives)
- Lipophility: atenolol, nadolol and sotalol are water soluble; but other β-blockers are more lipophilic so they have higher CNS penetration, and therefore they can more likely cause vivid dreams/nightmares. Therefore if a patient on β-blockers has started experiencing vivid dreams/nightmares, it may likely be related to the medication and changes to atenolol, nadolol or sotalol can be considered
- Elimination route: Atenolol and nadolol are excreted renally so patient with renal insufficiency should have lower dosages

GENERAL SIDE EFFECTS

- β-blockers can cause bradycardia, conduction abnormalities, acute heart failure (HF)

CAUTION

- ! Abrupt discontinuation of β-blockers can produce myocardial infarction, unstable angina, or even death especially in patients with coronary disease. Hence, slow reductions is advised over a period of at least 1 or 2 weeks

α1- RECEPTOR BLOCKERS

Doxazosin, prazosin

- α1-receptor blockers act by inhibiting catecholamine uptake by α1 receptors in the smooth muscle of peripheral vasculature, leading to its relaxation and vasodilation:
  ↓ systemic vascular resistance (SVR)
  ↓ BP
- Orthostatic hypotension may occur potentially due to sudden BP drop – accompanying signs can be present such as dizziness or fainting, palpitations and even syncope
- Na^+ and H_2O retention can also appear so α1-receptor blockers used chronically should be given together with diuretics to minimize risk of edema
- For HT, α1-receptor blockers should only be given with first-line antihypertensives
- Men with benign prostatic hyperplasia is a particular situation for which α1-receptor blockers can be reserved.

STAGE 3

HYPERTENSION

STAGE BY STAGE LEARNING PATH

STAGE 1
BP CONCEPTS AND HT PATHOPHYSIOLOGY

↓

STAGE 2
DIFFERENT CLASSES OF ANTIHYPERTENSIVE DRUGS

↓

STAGE 3
CLINICAL GUIDELINES ON HT TREATMENT

↓

STAGE 4
DRUGS OF CHOICE WHEN CONCOMITANT DISEASES

↓

STAGE 5
DRUGS OF CHOICE FOR SPECIAL POPULATIONS

J. CONSTANTINO

HYPERTENSION

STAGE 3

CLINICAL GUIDELINES ON HT TREATMENT

TREATMENT GOALS

HT MANAGEMENT

WHAT DO THE GUIDELINES SAY

+ **COMPLEMENTARY VIDEOS ON YOUTUBE**

Clinical guidelines, guides on treatment, treatment guidance, no matter what you want to call it...

Now that the main classes of antihypertensive drugs are covered and explained, it is important to understand what the treatment goals are for HT and how clinically these drugs are used – what do the guidelines say on lines of treatment?

In this chapter 3, we are going through the first 'general' guidance on lines of treatment for HT. Let's say it applies to the general population if there are no other associated diseases or patients are part of a special population. So this should be what applies for the simpler scenarios.

However it should be understood that HT treatment is also very dependent on concomitant diseases and the individual patient (special populations should be carefully considered). So that is the reason why on chapter 4 and 5, drugs of choice are discussed when certain conditions are present and special populations are being treated.

But firstly, it is very important you understand the simpler scenarios so we can move forward to those complementary notes.

LET'S GET STARTED!

TREATMENT GOALS

HT is a **MAJOR RISK FACTOR** for many **CONDITIONS**:

STROKE

MI

CHRONIC KIDNEY DISEASE

HEART FAILURE

PERIPHERAL VASCULAR DISEASE

COGNITIVE DECLINE

PREMATURE DEATH

↓ therefore:

HT is one of the most preventable causes of morbidity and mortality.

↓ then:

OVERALL GOAL
↓ morbidity & ↓ mortality

Certain conditions such as DM, kidney problems and CAD determine the specific target goals for BP values.

Values regarding BP goals are specified below:

BP GOALS	BP (mmHg)
Patients with DM / Chronic kidney disease / CAD	↓ 130/80
Any other patients	↓ 140/90

In other words, generally BP target is below 140/90, however **guidelines specify stricter BP treatment goals** for patients with **DM, kidney disease or CAD** (coronary artery disease) - which should be **below 130/80.**

ALSO Treatment of BP is extremely important if:

- BP is persistently ↑ **160/100 mmHg**
- **CV risk** or existing **vascular disease**
- **Target organ damage** (e.g. brain, kidney, heart, retina) with BP ↑ 140/90 mmHg.

Reduce BP slowly – as **rapid reduction of BP can be fatal**, especially in context of an acute stroke.

> **!**
>
> **NOT TO FORGET -** Two very important factors (further in detail – in stage 4 and stage 5 of the book) should be carefully taken into account to choose most appropriate drug treatment of antihypertensive therapy:
>
> 1) **Concomitant conditions**
>
> 2) **Special populations**

HYPERTENSION MANAGEMENT: WHAT DO THE GUIDELINES SAY

HT is a complex disease!

So, its treatment and management is in constant update due to new results of ongoing studies.

Taking into account the recent evidence presented on '**NICE guidelines on Hypertension in adults: diagnosis and management**', we will look into 4 steps to consider for HT treatment.

HT TREATMENT CONSISTS OF 4 STEPS TO FOLLOW

Step 1 (One drug):

- **Patients aged ↓ 55 year: offer ACE INHIBITOR or ARB** if ACE inhibitor not tolerated (for example, due to cough)

- **Patients aged ↑ or 55 years / Black: offer CCB or THIAZIDE-LIKE DIURETIC*** if CCB not tolerated (due to peripheral oedema) or concurrent heart failure condition.

↓

Step 2 (Two drugs):

If BP not controlled, offer both above: **ACE INHIBITOR or ARB** if ACE inhibitor not tolerated + **CCB or THIAZIDE-LIKE DIURETIC** if CCB not tolerated

---

*THIAZIDE-LIKE DIURETIC such as chlorthalidone or indapamide in preference to conventional thiazide diuretics - bendroflumethiazide/hydrochlorthiazide. However, if BP is already controlled with bendroflumethiazide / hydrochlorthiazide, these should be maintained.

↓

Step 3 (Three drugs):

- **If BP not controlled,** review meds of step 2 and ensure treatment is optimal. Then if so, consider **combination of following 3 drugs**: ACE INHIBITOR / ARB + CCB + THIAZIDE-LIKE DIURETIC

↓

Step 4 (four drugs):

For cases of 'resistant HT'

- **If BP not controlled with 3 drugs,** consider adding a **4th drug** of the following: Low dose SPIRONOLACTONE or higher dose THIAZIDE-LIKE DIURETIC
  Or alternatively, α-BLOCKER or β-BLOCKER

HYPERTENSION MANAGEMENT: GUIDELINES
REVIEW OF MAIN POINTS

Does it make sense? Let's view it once again in the form of tables (below). Take it as a summary of these **NICE guidelines** on **HT Management**.

STEP 1 depends on age:

Patients aged ↓ 55 year

ACE INHIBITOR or ARB if ACE inhibitor not tolerated (e.g. cough)

Patients aged ↑ or 55 years / Black

CCB or THIAZIDE-LIKE DIURETIC

if CCB not tolerated (due to peripheral oedema) or concurrent HF

STEP 2

If BP still not controlled – STEP 2
Offer both above:

ACE INHIBITOR or ARB if ACE inhibitor not tolerated

+

CCB or THIAZIDE-LIKE DIURETIC if CCB not tolerated

STEP 3

If BP not controlled – STEP 3
Review meds of step 2 and ensure treatment is optimal

If so, consider **combo of 3 drugs**:

ACE INHIBITOR or ARB

+

CCB

+

THIAZIDE-LIKE DIURETIC

If BP not controlled with 3 drugs – STEP 4

Consider adding a **4th drug** of the following:

Low dose SPIRONOLACTONE or higher dose THIAZIDE-LIKE DIURETIC

Or alternatively,

α-BLOCKER or β-BLOCKER

Review these tables and come back to these section as many times as you need to keep it in mind.

Review is key!

STAGE 4

HYPERTENSION

STAGE BY STAGE LEARNING PATH

STAGE 1
BP CONCEPTS AND **HYPERTENSION PATHOPHYSIOLOGY**

↓

STAGE 2
DIFFERENT CLASSES OF **ANTIHYPERTENSIVE DRUGS**

↓

STAGE 3
CLINICAL GUIDELINES ON TREATMENT LINES

↓

STAGE 4
DRUGS OF CHOICE WHEN **CONCOMITANT DISEASES**

↓

STAGE 5
DRUGS OF CHOICE FOR **SPECIAL POPULATIONS**

J. CONSTANTINO

HYPERTENSION

STAGE 4

DRUGS OF CHOICE
WHEN CONCOMITANT DISEASES

HEART FAILURE (HF)

POST-MI

CAD - CORONARY ARTERY DISEASE

DIABETES

CKD - CHRONIC KIDNEY DISEASE

STROKE PREVENTION

+ **COMPLEMENTARY VIDEOS ON YOUTUBE**

Other conditions matter!

Now that the first 'general' guidance on lines of treatment is seen. We learnt what applies to the general population if there are no other associated diseases or patients are part of a special population.

However as mentioned, it should be noted that HT treatment is also very dependent on concomitant diseases and the individual patient (special populations should be carefully considered). Then, on this chapter 4 because drugs of choice can vary when patients display certain conditions guidance on this particular situation is going to be given.

LET'S GET STARTED!

CONCOMITANT CONDITIONS

Antihypertensive drugs should be chosen taken into account the patient diseases. As mentioned before certain conditions determine that specific antihypertensive drugs are given preferably.

Hence, there are drugs of choice for the following conditions:

Heart Failure (HF)

Post-MI

CAD - Coronary Artery Disease

Diabetes

CKD - Chronic Kidney Disease

Stroke Prevention

Heart Failure (HF)

ACE INHIBITOR + DIURETIC + β-BLOCKER + ALDOSTERONE ANTAGONIST (SPIRONOLACTONE)

- **ACE inhibitor + Diuretic** constitute the first-line therapy to help managing left ventricular (LF) dysfunction which is characteristic in patients with HF.
  ACE inhibitors have cardio-protective effects by reverting the left ventricular dysfunction and consequently ↓CV morbidity & ↓mortality. ARBs can be used as alternative therapy when there is intolerance to ACE inhibitors or as add-on treatment for those with 3-drug combination.
  Diuretics are good at relieving symptoms, such as oedema (loop diuretics like furosemide are first choice especially in patients with advanced HF).

- **β-blockers** are also beneficial for LV dysfunction. It is important that low doses with gradual increase are carefully adopted to avoid HF exacerbation.

- **Aldosterone antagonists** are a good drug class to combine in addition to the previous ones – particularly beneficial when furosemide is taken by patient. Spironolactone acts as potassium-sparing diuretic to balance K^+ excretion promoted by furosemide.

However, if **aldosterone antagonists** are combined with **ARBs** hyperkalaemia (↑ K^+) may occur so concomitant use is not recommended → and if both agents are combined then close K^+ monitoring should be performed.

Post-MI

β-BLOCKER + ACE INHIBITOR / ARB

- **β-blockers** are responsible for ↓adrenergic stimulation on heart, and therefore ↓ risk of subsequent myocardial infarction (MI) or sudden cardiac death

- **ACE inhibitors / ARBs** are known to be cardioprotective (as also mentioned for HF), and improve cardiac function and consequently ↓ risk of CV events after MI.

CAD - Coronary Artery Disease

β-BLOCKER + ACE INHIBITOR / ARB + CCB / DIURETIC

- **β-blockers** are standard therapy in patients with stable angina acting by
    ↓ BP
    ↓ O_2 demand (improving myocardial function)

- **ACE inhibitors** combined with **β-blockers** are first choice for acute coronary diseases, as both drug classes have additive effect at:
    ↓ BP
    ↓ acute ischemia
    ↓ CV risk

- **CCBs** are used as alternatives to/or associated with **β-blockers** to control stable angina:
Non-dihydropyridine CCBs (verapamil and diltiazem) are used often as alternative drug to stable agina; whereas dihydropyridines CCBs are often used as add-on to the therapy.

- **Diuretics** (such as thiazides) may be added to promote additional:
    ↓ BP
    ↓ CV risk

Diabetes

ACE INHIBITOR / ARB + DIURETIC + CCB / β-BLOCKER

- **ACE inhibitors / ARBs** are known not only for providing cardioprotection (↓ CV risk), but also nephropotection, thus diabetic patients with high BP* should be prescribed with one of these drug classes.

> *** KEY NOTE**
> As mentioned previously, **BP target goal for patient with Diabetes is lower (↓130/ 80 mmHg)** than to population with no diabetes or other concomitant diseases.

- **Diuretics** (such as thiazide diuretics) are recommended as 2nd drug to promote additional:
    ↓ BP
    ↓ CV risk

- **CCBs** can also be added as 3rd drug to control HT in patients with diabetes, and nondihydropyridine CCBs (verapamil and diltiazem) may provide higher renal protective effects than dihydropyridine CCBs as per some studies

- **β-blockers**, alternatively, can also be used as 3ʳᵈ drug to control HT especially for patients with post-MI.

    It should be considered however that symptoms of hypoglycaemia can be masked by β-blockers (tremor, tachycardia and palpitations) as they slow the heart rate. If these considerations are taken into account, β-blockers are overall safe for use in diabetic patients.

CKD - Chronic Kidney Disease

ACE INHIBITOR / ARB

- **ACE inhibitors / ARBs** are the 1st line to manage HT in patients with CKD due to their known **nephroprotective** effects.

Stroke Prevention

ACE INHIBITOR + DIURETIC

- **ACE inhibitors + (Thiazide) diuretic** is a combination that have shown to reduce the incidence of recurrent stroke in patients with history of ischemic stroke.

J. CONSTANTINO

STAGE 5

J. CONSTANTINO

HYPERTENSION

STAGE BY STAGE LEARNING PATH

STAGE 1
BP CONCEPTS AND **HYPERTENSION PATHOPHYSIOLOGY**

↓

STAGE 2
DIFFERENT CLASSES OF **ANTIHYPERTENSIVE DRUGS**

↓

STAGE 3
CLINICAL GUIDELINES ON TREATMENT LINES

↓

STAGE 4
DRUGS OF CHOICE WHEN **CONCOMITANT DISEASES**

↓

STAGE 5
DRUGS OF CHOICE FOR **SPECIAL POPULATIONS**

J. CONSTANTINO

HYPERTENSION

STAGE 5

DRUGS OF CHOICE
FOR SPECIAL POPULATION

- OLDER PEOPLE
- CHILDREN & ADOLESCENT
- PREGNANT WOMEN
- AFRICAN

+ **COMPLEMENTARY VIDEOS ON YOUTUBE**

Finally, always make patient-centred decisions!

Some patients are part of a special population.

Antihypertensive drugs should be chosen taken into account the not only the concomitant patient diseases as discussed on the stage 4, BUT ALSO SPECIAL POPULATIONS. Certain populations determine indeed specific antihypertensive drugs to be given preferably.

Hence, there are drugs of choice for the following population types

SPECIAL POPULATIONS

Older People

Children & Adolescent

Pregnant women

African

LET'S GET STARTED!

OLDER PEOPLE

DIURETICS / ACE INHIBITOR / ARB (for all, smaller than usual doses should be initially used)

- Safer options for elderly people are **Diuretics** & also **ACE inhibitors / ARBs** and provide better benefits, according to studies. However it important to note that initial doses should be smaller than normal due to pathophysiologic modifications older people display.

- It is interesting that the higher systolic BP, the higher morbidity and mortality seems to be - so it is vital to make sure isolated systolic HT is always carefully treated, as well as both systolic and diastolic elevated BP.

CHILDREN & ADOLESCENT

ACE INHIBITOR(*) / ARB(*) / β-BLOCKERS / CCBs / THIAZIDE-TYPE DIURETICS

(*) CI in ♀ sexually active

Before going any further, it is crucial to bear in mind that: younger people suffer more commonly from secondary HT than adults – being **kidney disease the most common cause for secondary HT.** ↓

PRIMARY	SECONDARY
> 90 % of cases	< 10% of cases
CAUSE: Unknown Results from an underlying pathophysiologic mechanism of unknown cause.	CAUSE: Underlying known condition(s) are present increasing the blood pressure: **Chronic kidney disease or renovascular disease** are the most common. Other possible ones are Cushing's syndrome, pheochromocytoma, obstructive sleep apnea, primary hyperaldosteronism & hyperthyroidism.

- **ACE inhibitors / ARBs** are known for their nephroprotective effects (as mentioned before) so they are the 1ˢᵗ line to consider in cases of secondary HT due to kidney disease.

However, they are contraindicated in girls who are sexually active due to potential teratogenicity.

- **β-blockers, CCBs, Thiazide-type diuretics** are also acceptable drug choices especially in cases of ♀ sexually active.

- On other hand, for other cases besides the most common secondary HT:
Non-pharmacological measures (such as weight loss and diet changes) are the first therapy – for cases of primary HT in children and adolescents – especially those suffering from obesity.

PREGNANCY

METHYLDOPA / β-BLOCKERS (LABETALOL) / NIFEDIPINE

(ACE INHIBITORs/ARB not to be used because they are are teratogen drugs)

First of all, there are 3 ≠ possible situations to consider where HT is present in pregnancy: 1) chronic HT, 2) preeclampsia, and 3) eclampsia.

- 1) **Chronic HT** refers to high BP present **even before** the pregnancy started;

- 2) **Preeclampsia** refers to cases of BP ↑140/90 **after** 20 weeks of pregnancy

- 3) Preeclampsia in its turn can involve to **eclampsia** which is considered a medical emergency where pregnant women suffer convulsions.

- For the first scenario: **1) Chronic HT:**
Metildopa is the drug of choice as it is widely used (long time experience). Also, **β-blockers**(such as labetalol), and **CCBs** can be acceptable drug choices especially in cases of ♀ sexually active.

x ACE inhibitors or ARBs are completely contraindicated as mentioned previously

- Then, for **2) preeclampsia** & **3) eclampsia:**
The unique definitive treatment is considered **delivery**. Until no eclampsia is present, treatment management implies **low activity, more rest** and **strict monitoring** since it is a serious and delicate situation

AFRICAN BACKGROUND

THIAZIDE-TYPE DIURETICS & CCBs (β-BLOCKERS / ACE INHIBITORs / ARBs provide ↑ antihypertensive effect)

- Due to physiological ≠ces (mainly in terms of mechanisms of transport, Na^+ secretion, BP response to volume changes, glomerular filtration etc), management of BP in African should be adapted.

- **Thiazide-type diuretics** are first line for most patients; should be combined with a second drug, being **CCBs** the more effective usually. Also, significant and ↑ antihypertensive effect is obtained when either of them (thiazides/CCBs) are combined with β-blockers / ACE Inhibitors / ARBs.

REVIEW

↓

DRUGS OF CHOICE

CONCOMITANT DISEASES & FOR SPECIAL POPULATIONS

Lastly to review stage 4 and 5, see the next tables that summarise information on impact of **coexisting conditions** and **special populations** in the chosen antihypertensive treatment,

CONCOMITANT CONDITIONS

HEART FAILURE

ACE INHIBITOR + DIURETIC
+
B-BLOCKER
+
ALDOSTERONE ANTAGONIST
(SPIRONOLACTONE)

POST-MI

B-BLOCKER
+
ACE INHIBITOR / ARB

CAD

B-BLOCKER
+
ACE INHIBITOR / ARB
+
CCB OR DIURETIC

DIABETES

ACE INHIBITOR / ARB
+
DIURETIC
+
CCB / B-BLOCKER

STROKE PREVENTION

ACE INHIBITOR
+
DIURETIC

SPECIAL POPULATIONS

OLDER PEOPLE

DIURETICS

ACE INHIBITOR / ARB

!

Smaller than usual doses should be initially used

CHILDREN & ADOLESCENT

ACE INHIBITOR (*) / ARB (*)

β-BLOCKERS

CCBs

THIAZIDE-TYPE DIURETICS

(*) CI in ♀ sexually active

PREGNANCY

METHYLDOPA

β-BLOCKERS (LABETALOL)

CCB (NIFEDIPINE)

AFRICAN

THIAZIDE DIURETICS

& CCBs

Also: β-BLOCKERS / ACE INHIBITORs / ARBs provide ↑antihypertensive effect

LATER NOTES ON ANTIHYPERTENSIVE DRUGS

CONGRATULATIONS!

You have made it to this stage so after all this reading I gathered some final complementary notes or facts I'd like you to add to your current knowledge so far.

- **! Antihypertensive drugs are NOT recommended in the acute phase of ischaemic stroke**

    WHY? When patient suffers ischaemic stroke the cerebral blood supply to brain was limited, and antihypertensive drugs can reduce even more the cerebral blood perfusion.

- **β-blockers are not completely CI in diabetic patients, but they can mask hypoglycaemia symptoms.**

    HOW? Physiological response to hypoglycaemia (low levels of glucose) involves symptoms such as tachycardia, increased heart rate. However β-blockers reduce the heart rate.

ARE THERE ANY OTHER HYPOGLYCEMIA SIGNS CAN BE DETECTED IN PATIENTS ON β-BLOCKERS?

Physiological response to hypoglycaemia (low levels of glucose) can also involve sweating, and β-blockers do NOT block sweating so this may be one of the few alerting signs of hypoglycaemia in patients on β-blockers.

When patient suffers ischaemic stroke the cerebral blood supply to brain is limited, and antihypertensive drugs can reduce even more the cerebal blood perfusion.

- **Thiazides and thiazide-like diuretics are also vasodilators.**

- Avoid thiazides in patients with diabetes, gout, and renal impairment, they can make these conditions worsen.

- **For malignant hypertension use oral therapy, unless there is encephalopathy or CCF.** The aim is for a *controlled* reduction in BP over days, not hours.

- β-blockers are no longer recommended as first-line therapy for HT, but they may be considered as initial therapy in younger patients who cannot tolerate ACE inhibitors or ARBs, in ♀ of child-bearing age, or in people with sympathetic drive. β-blockers are also considered in patients with resistant HT.

NOT A GOODBYE BUT A
SEE YOU LATER.

J. CONSTANTINO

USED AND USEFUL REFERENCES

NICE guidelines → https://www.nice.org.uk/guidance

& https://pathways.nice.org.uk/pathways/hypertension

BOOKS:

Pharmacotherapy Handbook - Barbara Wells, Joseph DiPiro, Terry Schwinghammer, Cecily DiPiro-McGraw-Hill Medical (2014)

Oxford Handbook Of Clinical Pharmacy - Philip Wiffen, Marc Mitchell, Melanie Snelling, Nicola Stoner - Oxford Medical Handbooks - Oxford University Press (2017)

CANVA for images design → https://www.canva.com

ACKNOWLEDGMENTS

I am truly grateful to these people who somehow contributed for this Book to be created.

My dear friends **Ana Coelho** and **Paulo Carrasqueira** - for keeping my dedication and motivation higher on a daily basis. They must have a super power.

The **Prof Isabel Vitória** from Faculty of Pharmacy of the University of Coimbra, my Professor of Pharmacology & an inspiration in the academy - for discussing ideas at writing books.

My partner **Gabriela** - for constantly being supportive, attentive, & being completely extraordinary.

Pedro, my brother - who gave me excellent insights on how to make this book even more intuitive, visual & having its own entity.

Sandra & Diamantino, my parents - who follow my career since the very beginning and provide full support by any means since day one.

ON A FINAL NOTE,

I would like to **THANK YOU** for choosing this book to help improving your knowledge on the cardiovascular system.

I hope I could positively impact on your learning, and pass on the information in an easy & appealing way so that you **don't forget it easily** as that was my ultimate goal.

↓

If so, I would like to encourage you to take a few minutes to leave a **quick review on Amazon** so other potential readers know what to expect from this book.

Any kind of insights / opinion you have may help me to comprehend if I fulfilled your expectations, refine the content for future editions and future publications, and let the potential readers understand whether this one can be a 'good fit' for them and what they need or not.

@

Feel free to email me any queries or thoughts
joaomrc@hotmail.com

I will do my best to reply as soon as I can.

ABOUT THE AUTHOR

YES, the template I'm using wants a bit more about the author, SO:

I am a Portuguese Pharmacist (YES, from that small country attached to Spain. I do speak Portuguese too, I do love Portuguese food and I play football almost as well as Cristiano Ronaldo does but I have decided to become a Pharmacist).

Currently I am working in England as pharmacist.
I studied in the University of Coimbra, Portugal and became officially a Pharmacist in 2014 thanks to the Faculty of Pharmacy. This city, Coimbra, is surely one the best city for students in the world & taught me way more than being a pharmacist, gave me loads of work & studies to focus on - but also joy, parties and fun to be entertained with. Taught me we have time to accomplish every little thing we wish, all we need is a good balance of focus & discipline. It brought me most of my best friends and partner.
Connected me to a new world.

WHAT DOES BEING A PHARMACIST MEAN TO ME?
It means to me being professional and rational enough to evaluate accurately & wholly each case as a unique case, but at the same time emotional enough to understand how you can help your patient and go beyond the norm. No matter what other pharmacist would do, just do your best. You can know it all but if you do not use in the patient's interest it's

worth nothing.
The smallest advice can MAKE A BIG DIFFERENCE for others.
The smallest dream or goal of yours can the BIGGEST IMPACT ON OTHERS.

SO ON THIS VERY FINAL NOTE
GO BEYOND THE NORM & EVEN SURPRISE YOURSELF.
If you can do so on a daily basis,
you may well become the Ronaldo of the Pharmaceutical World.

J. CONSTANTINO

EASY PEASY PHARMACOLOGY | HYPERTENSION

I DID
READ, WRITE,
DRAW, LEARN,
FILM, WATCH,
TALK OUT LOUD
LISTEN,
THINK,
RELAX, REPEAT

J. CONSTANTINO

P. S.
I DID HAVE FUN TOO DEVELOPING THIS WORK FOR YOU

I HOPE YOU ENJOYED IT TOO

STAY TUNNED

MORE BOOKS LIKE THIS ONE ARE ON ITS WAY.

J. CONSTANTINO

#easypeasy
#PHARMACOLOGY

#EASYPEASYPHARMACOLOGY

Do not forget to leave me your review & thoughts

MANY THANKS ONCE AGAIN!

Printed in Great Britain
by Amazon